CORSH
BORN AND BRED 2

Including 32 Pages in Full Colour

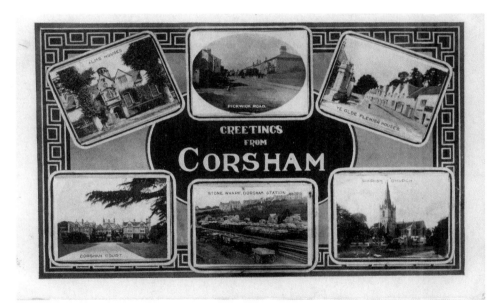

Corsham Multiview c.1920

To My Family

CORSHAM
BORN AND BRED 2

A Portrait in Old Picture Postcards

By

Stephen Flavin

British Library Cataloguing in Publication Data
Flavin, Stephen.
Corsham Born and Bred 2

A catalogue record for this book is available from the British Library

ISBN 0 9553382 0 4
ISBN 978 0 9553382 0 5

Printed by Anthony Rowe Limited
Chippenham Wiltshire 2006

CONTENTS

Acknowledgements vi
Preface vii
The Picture Postcard: An Outline History ix

1. The Road to Corsham 1

2. The Road to Pickwick 23

3. Pickwick, Hartham and Biddestone 35

4. To Corsham Court 57

5. The Road to Lacock and Gastard 75

6. To the Railway Station 95

7. The Road to Neston 105

Front cover: Comic Postcard c. 1910
Back Cover: Corsham High Street c. 1905
Title Page: Methuen Coat of Arms reproduced by kind permission of James Methuen-Campbell: argent, three wolves heads erased, proper, borne on the breast of an imperial eagle. Supporters: two fiery lynxes reguardant proper, collared and lined or. The Latin motto *"Virtus Invidiae Scopus"* means, "Virtue is the Mark of Envy".

ACKNOWLEDGEMENTS

I should like to extend my gratitude to the following people who have contributed to this book. First and foremost to my wife Sue and my children, Grace, Michael and Martha to whom this book is dedicated. Without their constant interest and support, this book would not have been possible.

James Methuen-Campbell	Corsham Court
Canon Roger Clifton	St. Bartholomew's Church
Clive Hancock	Local History
Joe James	Local History
Tom Gale	Military Information
Richard Pugh	Imaging and Set-up
Antony Rowe	Printers

Every attempt has been made to ensure that the information contained herein is accurate. I would like to apologise in advance for any errors which may have inadvertently crept in.

To view the whole collection or to purchase additional copies of this and other books online visit www.corshampostcards.com

PREFACE

I published my first book *Corsham Born and Bred* in 1991. It has taken fifteen years, and the encouragement of my friends, family and those who enjoyed the first book, to convince me that a second book was needed. If you enjoy this book and would like additional copies, then contact mail@corshampostcards.com

A number of elderly folk who contributed to the first book are sadly no longer with us including the late John, 6th Lord Methuen (1925-1994). My first book successfully achieved its primary aim of recording for posterity what it was like to live and grow up in a small rural town at the start of the 20th century.

Corsham Born and Bred 2 is similar to the first book, in that it creates an historical journey through the town and its neighbouring villages. The unique images from my private collection are arranged in geographical order. In 1991, I had 600 postcards. I now have over 2000, which makes it the largest known collection of Edwardian postcards of Corsham in the world! There are still more to collect and you may be able to help add to this historical collection. If you have any old photographs or postcards of Corsham, then simply email a message or an image to mail@corshampostcards.com. It is my intention to make this publication part of a series in order that those with a keen interest in Corsham and its social history can build their own collection. If you enjoy this book then simply visit the website and reserve your copy of the next instalment planned for 2007.

Corsham Born and Bred 2 differs in several significant ways from the first. There are more images to enjoy and each is supported by a brief description. The major difference is that each image is connected to hundreds more images on a unique website called www.corshampostcards.com. This website contains my entire collection and is updated as other postcards of Corsham are added. *Corsham Born and Bred 2* is interactive and allows those with the Internet to add information and images. These books and the website have allowed me to share my passion for Corsham postcards and my love of this unique West Country English town.

I finish this preface in the same way I did fifteen years ago:

It is my sincere desire that through this publication I will be able to share my enjoyment of Corsham's intimate history as shown on picture postcards. It is written for everyone with an interest in the past, and particularly for those who with affection, know Corsham in Wiltshire simply as home.

Stephen Flavin 2006

THE PICTURE POSTCARD

A Brief History

The first plain postcards appeared in Austria in 1869. The following year postcards were produced in Britain. However, it was not until 1894 that postcards began to include a picture on one of the faces. Until 1902 all postcards had to carry the message on the front and the address on the back. On January 1st 1902, Britain became the first country to divide the back thus permitting both the message and the address on the same side. This coincided with the introduction of standard size: 5.5 x 3.5 inches and the result was an explosion in the manufacture of picture postcards.

Between 1902 and 1914 there was a boom in the popularity of postcards. In 1906 an estimated 264 million postcards were sent in this country and between 1894 and 1918, 2,500 million had been posted. At first collecting postcards was the pastime of middle-class young ladies. Mass production made it possible for men as well as women from every social position to join in with what was rapidly becoming a national craze.

Why was the Edwardian postcard so successful? Essentially it was the cheapest and most reliable means of communication before the advent of telephone. In some ways it was like email or text messaging is today. The Golden Age of postcards had taken place when a great deal of entertainment was still home based; before the visual revolution of cinema and television. Even newspapers were restricted by the amount of pictorial information they carried. By 1908 postcard sales in this country had started to decline. The weekly outing to 'the flicks' and the increased ownership of the camera culminated in a growing disinterest in the picture postcard.

Postcards were produced in several different ways. Small, local firms reproduced cards from an original in small batches. The quality of the copy was determined by the skill of the photographer in the developing process. The caption on the front of the card was often a handwritten addition. Many hundreds of postcards and photographs depicting life in and around Corsham can be attributed to Herbert Spackman who had a small studio behind the family shop in the High Street. Regional companies, such as R. Wilkinson of Trowbridge, used a mass production technique involving contact printing from a negative onto machines which could produce copies in large numbers. These cards often depict standard stereotypical views of the parish church, large houses, the High Street and other notable landmarks. There were also national postcard publishers such as Francis Frith, Judges and Valentines to name but three. The Frith Company succeeded in producing postcards of virtually every town and village in the country including Corsham.

It is the work of the local photographers such as Herbert Spackman of Corsham which is of most interest, since they were ideally placed to record shots of local events and personalities, of country lanes and local disasters. These rare, 'real photographic' postcards have become the 'Cartes Supremes' to the modern day postcard enthusiast.

This brief history of the Edwardian picture postcard provides an important perspective to the postcards which have been reproduced here. As a result of natural wastage over a hundred years, many of the cards in this collection, especially those produced in small quantities, are unique.

Edwardian Romance! This couple embrace passionately under a signpost to Corsham with caption: *"Much too busy to write beyond Corsham agrees with me."* Cards identical to this would have been produced for a number of towns with the name in the sign changed to suit. This particular card was franked in Corsham post-office in 1908. It was used for the cover of the first book *'Corsham Born and Bred'* 1991 by Stephen Flavin.

THE ROAD TO CORSHAM

Corsham Born and Bred 2 follows the same pattern as its predecessor in providing a journey in picture postcards through this small West Country town and its surrounding villages. It is a fascinating place, full of character and brimming over with rustic charm. A journey through Corsham is a journey through history itself.

This is a real photographic postcard of the Cross Keys taken in 1929. This is an ancient crossroads. The road in view is the Great London Road (A4) towards Chippenham. Notice the horse drawn carriage. The stone tiled roof cottage (left) date-back to the 17th Century. A single gas lamp (centre) adds to the quaint rural atmosphere. The washing line in the garden suggests a Monday!

The Cross Keys Inn. This superb photograph captures life in Corsham in the 1920's. The wooden signpost at this crossroads (left) directs traffic to Bath, Chippenham, Biddestone village and Corsham Station. This was a relatively safe place to stand (not now!).

The Flemish Houses on a postcard sent in 1904. Postcards of Corsham before this year are rare; the earliest in this collection is dated 1902. The cobbled path (left) has survived to this day and this scene is instantly recognisable to locals. Notice the approaching horse drawn cart. The square fronted building (right) was the Caxton Printing Works from where Lewin Spackman produced many Corsham postcards. The shadow would make the time of day approximately midday!

Flemish Buildings, Corsham

A view of the Flemish Houses in 1910 by W.R.H. Ray. Published by F.J. Bryant. A public meeting on July 29th 1896 agreed to erect a memorial fountain to the late Charles Mayo (left). The fountain was for use by foot passengers and cattle! It was to stand 'as an appreciation of the valuable services he consistently rendered to Corsham'. The small bell-tower on the roofline remains from the town's first fire station c. 1820.

Corsham, Flemish Houses.

A busy street scene near the famous Flemish Houses. This postcard c.1907 shows the Mayo fountain. A group of children stand by it. A horse drawn delivery cart adds to the rustic feel of this quiet moment from Corsham's past. A small saddlers and harness-maker's shop (right) was run by Tidmarsh and Kibble.

3

Town Hall and High Street, Corsham.

View of the High Street southwards. The appearance as a painting (see back cover) was created by adding the colour onto a negative of a photograph before colour photography. The Town Hall with clock (1897) is prominent. J.E. Eastman's hardware store on the left became the town's post office. Bicyclists and a horse-drawn cart show Corsham life in 1915.

Philip Mountbatten takes the salute at the Town Hall as the band march by. The Prince became engaged to Princess Elizabeth whilst stationed at the H.M.S. Royal Arthur Naval Base in Corsham in 1949. This looks like a wet November 11th Remembrance Sunday. Wilkins Corn Store is visible right of Town Hall.

4

The Town Hall on a photograph from c.1947. Notice the cars (now vintage). This appears to have been taken on a cold spring day. The side entrance to the Town Hall (far right) led to a coffee tavern. It has since been blocked up. The Pack Horse Inn is in the centre of this postcard.

This postcard of the Town Hall was sent from the Post Office on September 25th 1905. It was bought from Francis Baines' chemist in the High Street. The horse cart probably belonged to Flint's Bakery.

A rare internal shot of the Town Hall during the First World War when it was the Voluntary Aid Detachment (VAD) Hospital. Notice the Christmas decorations. Several soldiers are in beds (left). This postcard was discovered in Canada. Fortunately someone wrote December 25th 1916 Corsham Hospital on the back!

Photographic postcard by Herbert Spackman. Hospital Group no.5 September 15th, 1915. Hundreds of soldiers were treated here, many with severe injuries and diseases resulting from the early years of the Great War (1914-18). Volunteer nurses tended to their needs. The Town Hall was the Headquarters of the Red Cross in the area. At this time there were 30 beds. Officers stayed in a house opposite.

A large crowd have gathered outside the Town hall including several clergymen, nurses and Lady Methuen. The Baptist Minister, Pastor Smith, is addressing the assembled company. Could this be the declaration of peace at the end of WWI?

Superb event postcard taken in the High Street during the First World War. This photographic postcard was probably the work of Herbert Spackman. This appears to be a fundraising fete in aid of the Red Cross Hospital (Town Hall). Nurses and military figures mingle with local people to survey a fine array of home-grown produce and handcrafts with tables stretching as far as the Flemish houses.

The Town Hall, Pack Horse Inn and Eastmond's business are all clearly visible with the Flemish houses and the Mayo fountain in the background. The vehicle registration is MW 1037. The adverts (left) provide more information: the New Mixtures 1928 dates the card! Ronald Colman and Vilma Banky are appearing at the Palace Chippenham!

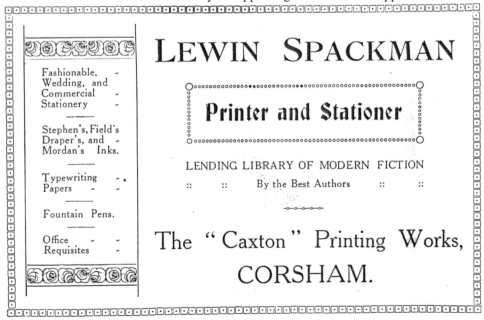

1925 advert for the Caxton Printing Works. This business was situated opposite the Flemish Houses. A number of postcards in this book, and others in the Stephen Flavin collection were produced by Lewin Spackman.

A stunning postcard by Herbert Spackman, which includes his image. On September 11th 1905, Spackman stood on the balcony of Matthew's shop and photographed troops returning from the war in South Africa. The Spackman and W. Fields shops are visible.

Spackman wrote to Johannes Friedrich in Esperanto: "*Very esteemed gentleman. I thank you for your very interesting postcard and I am replying with a photograph of my small town which I took myself and which shows my father's shop. The soldiers are coming for manoeuvres. I have also stuck on my own photograph and if it is convenient to you, I should be pleased to have one of yours. Corsham has about 4000 inhabitants and I am the only Esperantist*".

Postcard of the High Street outside the Royal Oak pub c.1931. The sign above the door advertises 'Teas with Hovis'. It was sold from E.H. Goddard's shop in Pickwick Road. Walter C. Oatley had a bicycle shop (left). Jack Wooton's hairdressing salon and the Cooperative Store (Co-op) are all left of centre. Behind Cheviot House was the Corsham Laundry (right).

The Royal Oak Hotel in the centre of the High Street c.1925. Advertising card, produced by Wadworths Brewery, Devizes. Hotel Proprietor F.G. Turner, Telephone 31. Notice also Corsham Dry-Cleaning and Dyeing Laundry (left) and Coates & Son Butchers delivery bicycle. In 1908 it was owned by the Anglo-Bavarian Brewery Company.

Arthur Matthews stands proudly outside his 'Bristol Drapery, Outfitting and Milliners' shop in the High Street. The windows are stacked with various linens. Note the three large gas lamps on the front of the shop. Arthur Matthews later moved to Bristol.

Real photographic postcard by Herbert Spackman. The scene is the centre of Lacock village. Perhaps Herbert Spackman was a guest. Miss Palmer must have been a noteworthy member of Lacock as the whole village is festooned with flags and bunting. The wedding was on June 11th 1908.

The Close, Corsham Park.

Pub. by F. Baines.

The Close is a tree-shaded path which connects the centre of the High Street with the Park on the Corsham Estate. It was variously known as Lovers Walk, John's Close, Janet's Close and the Drung! Notice the neat railings leading to a stile and the expanse of the Park. This postcard was sold from Francis Baines' Chemist Shop and posted from Bath in 1906. These railings have since been removed.

HIGH STREET, CORSHAM

The High Street towards The Grove and Pickwick Road. The fashion and cars help date this card. Lloyds Bank is on the right and T. Rees M.P.S. Chemist (left) selling Gilbeys Wines and Spirits. Other shops include Powell's Tobacconist and Ward & Son Drapery and Outfitting. In the distance there is an early branch of Tescos!

Corsham, Wilts.

An artist's drawing showing the High Street in the mid 1800's. The only named shop is SCOTT, which became Baines' chemist and afterwards, Rees Pharmacist. In the distance is The Grove.

13

One of the superb postcards which Herbert Spackman took to record the Coming of Age of Hon. Paul Methuen on September 30th 1907. The whole town was decked out in Union Jack flags, bunting and balloons. A banner above F. Baines chemist reads 'Many Happy Returns'. The window of the post office (right) displays postcards now in this collection 100 years on!

Six postcards show how Herbert Spackman recorded the Coming of Age of Hon. Paul Methuen on September 30th 1907. A banner near H. Spackman's shop reads 'Heaven Give You Many Happy Days'. Shops here include A. Hobbs, Saddlers and Caleb Davis' shoe shop.

The High Street in 1935. This is the only postcard in the Stephen Flavin collection which shows the Maternity Home. Caleb Davis' shoe shop is also clearly visible in this shot (right). The post office at this time, was situated next to the Maternity Home.

The High Street in 1905. A crowd have been immortalised, including the butchers of the Royal Wilts. The post office (right) was run by Fred J. Bryant. The post box (now bricked in) is still visible today. The house (extreme left) is Parkside, once home to the British composer Sir Michael Tippett. The card includes some early Corsham history.

Alfred Bird's Pastrycook and Confectioners shop in the High Street c.1910. Two women, presumably shop workers, stand outside. This shop stands on what was until recently Barclay's bank. Bottle collectors prize Alfred Bird Ginger Beer earthenware bottles. The window is full of chocolate and other sweet things! A blacksmith's shop, belonging to William Ring, stood behind this shop in the 1840's.

A shop front postcard showing Francis Baines, Stationer and Druggist. Postcards were sold from this shop and several appear in this collection. Collectors of old bottles (they exist!) are keen to find embossed bottles inscribed 'F. Baines Bottler Corsham' Mr Baines appears on the left. Francis Baines was a prominent member of Corsham society. In 1894 he was a founder member of the Town Council.

This postcard was bought from E.H. Goddard's shop in Pickwick Road. The vehicles and fashion suggest 1950. T. Ives Butchers promotes 'Bacon Curer'. H.R. James hardware shop in on the left. Just visible is P.E.G. Norman's, jeweller and watch repairer.

This is one of six postcards which Herbert Spackman took to record the Coming of Age of Hon. Paul Methuen on September 30th 1907. A procession through the town took place and ended with a presentation of a clock and other gifts outside the North Face of Corsham Court.

One of the best! Six postcards in this collection show how Herbert Spackman recorded the Coming of Age of Hon. Paul Methuen. Shops competed to produce the most impressive display. The sender writes *"The houses on the whole were decorated so pretty and looked so charming at night with fairy lights and Chinese lanterns."*

The south end of the High Street in 1907. The car was modern then! It is parked outside Cawte's garage which prominently displays bicycles. Crooks Milliners shop is opposite (left). Published on a postcard by F.H. S & Company, Bristol.

As Corsham's local photographer, Herbert Spackman was ideally placed to record events such as this one. The Church Choir outing to Wells, Cheddar and Burnham on 16th June 1913. This one shows two charabancs outside The Grove house.

A Stunning historical event recorded on these two postcards by Herbert Spackman on April 10th 1915. This is entitled Inspection of Scots Guards Corsham with soldiers standing at slope arms. Of particular interest is the backdrop which shows the entire frontage of 'Cawte Bros. Painters Plumbers and Engineers (telephone 10)'. The window contains adverts for Pratts Spirit and Moseley Tyres.

Postcard of the High Street at the point where it meets Pickwick Road. Shops of note here are J.H. Harding Grocers (Est. 1883), W. J. Evans and Cawtes Garage (right). The delivery van belonged to T. Ives the butcher. Can you spot the telephone box?

A busy street scene showing the Methuen Arms Hotel and Cawtes garage (left) in the High Street. The claim that this was established in 1417 may be an Edwardian exaggeration! Notice the Methuen Coat of Arms on the centre of the façade, where it still appears today. E.S. Ogburn was the proprietor. The card was sent during the First World War (1917) which accounts for the soldiers.

Corsham, The Grove.

The widest point of the High Street (south) as it meets Pickwick Road in 1907. Three ancient landmarks can be seen here. On the left is the side of Cawte and Sons, a garage started by Charles Cawte before 1900. The Methuen Arms Hotel and Grove House (facing) provide a scene very recognisable today. Sadly, Cawte's garage was demolished in the 1960's to create a car park.

Corsham.

Published by R. Wilkinson & Co., Trowbridge.

This postcard was sent in 1904. The detail on T.F. Harding, Grocer and Provision Merchant is fascinating. Each window advertises Cadbury's Cocoa. Also available was 'Spratt's Patent Puppy Biscuits'. Hardings was established in Corsham in 1889. Crooks Milliners is next door (centre) and Cawte's Plumbers and Decorators (right).

2. THE ROAD TO PICKWICK

Pickwick Road in 1905. The street is deserted apart from Mr Smallman (with bowler hat) from Bidddestone who is sign-writing above the 'Gardiner and Verity' milliners shop. J.H. Harding Grocers is on the right. A shaving sign juts out from Mr Goddard's Salon.

Pickwick Road in 1958. This distinctive row of shops has changed very little in the 50 years since this postcard was produced. Shops here include (right to left) Tobacconist, Cleverley Chemist, Pickwick Papers, Boots, and Bulsoms.

A group of banker masons gather for this photo by Herbert Spackman in 1910. The roofline of the High Street shops is visible in the background. Large blocks of oolite limestone were brought to the Town Yard from nearby stacking yards. These were fashioned into important and often ornate sculptures for buildings around the county, England and worldwide.

Corsham worked stone yard in 1920. This picture shows a team of banker masons at the Town Yard working blocks of quarried Bath Stone. The carved pieces shown are made to form columns for a church or cathedral. This area is now a shopping precinct car park.

Herbert Spackman was on hand to record the day when 10,000 soldiers marched through the town. This was taken outside Barnes' General Store in Pickwick Road. The central character rests on the brigade's drum. Identified as the Somerset Light Infantry. The gated entrance between the buildings led into the Town Stone Yard.

Pickwick Road in 1916. This assorted troupe appear to have just finished a show. Several are in 'drag'. Perhaps they were soldiers from the Town Hall (VAD) Hospital. Shops here include H.J. (Bert) Baines Confectioners, Arthur Little's Shoe Shop, 'The Pickwick Boot Stores', and 'Osmond' Hardware Shop.

British Red Cross Society and St John's Ambulance Association. This is the Corsham detachment on an original photographic postcard by Herbert Spackman. It appears that the Corsham detachment have won a cup. The names of these men, and the reason for the reward remain a mystery.

The Regal Cinema, Pickwick Road. The wooden garage (middle) belonged to Cawte's Brothers. Everything on this photograph from c.1950 has been demolished including the Victorian house (right).

W.F. Hancock Sentinel delivery lorry. Furniture removal and haulage contractors. Phone 93. Registration WV 5077. This unique postcard was taken at the sentinel factory in Shrewsbury where a photographic record was kept of each vehicle that they produced. The Hancock family have lived in Corsham for over 500 years.

The Wesleyan Church in Pickwick Road on a postcard from 1904, the year it was opened. The perimeter wall, railings and lamps have long since gone. In his opening address, Field Marshal Lord Methuen said *"I come to you today to congratulate you on that which you have, by God's gift been able to accomplish."*

Pickwick Road & Wesleyan Chapel, Corsham.

The Wesleyan Chapel and Corsham Conservative Club c.1910. This is a view of Pickwick Road looking west towards the village of Pickwick. On the right is the Wesleyan Church opened, in 1904. Corsham Conservatives, who originally met in Church Street, opened 'new' premises along with a flag pole (right). This is now part of Corsham Club.

CORSHAM BRITISH LEGION HUT. INTERIOR.

The interior of the British Legion on a postcard dating from 1912. The 'hut' stood in the same place as the current British Legion building. Access to this building was via 'The Golden Path' at the end of Post Office Lane. Notice the piano and several regulars, including a small girl. Sold by J. Hunter from his Teashop in the High Street.

Alexander Terrace in 1911. This view is from Pickwick Road looking north. At this time Alexander Terrace was a cul-de-sac. The trees in the background stood where Meriton Avenue was built in the 1930's. Note the delivery cart and absence of paths.

Corsham Town Band in the Recreation Ground, (see page 82). There was a bandstand here for some years until the vandals arrived! Although not named, there are probably members of the Hulbert, Gale, Rawlings and Simkins families here. This appears to have been taken during a fete. Photo by Castle Photos of Trowbridge.

Corsham, Pickwick Road.

Pickwick Road in 1905. The White Lion Pub, run by H. Badminton, is centre. The houses in this area are mostly detached, double-fronted Victorian dwellings which effectively joined Corsham with the nearby village of Pickwick.

The White Lion Pub on the corner of Paul Street and Pickwick Road (built c.1845). Mr H. Badminton is standing proudly at the entrance. The occasion is the Coronation of George V in 1911. The whole town joined the national celebrations with bunting, Union flags and balloons on display. The pub closed in the 1990's.

30

These soldiers are all Royal Artillery gunners, billeted in Corsham. This is the wedding of Mary Tanner (front row, middle). The Tanners lived in Paul Street. Had she married the rifle instructor on the left, identified as Laurie Grotton? He has inverted chevrons for long service and was wounded in action. The bride's parents, Mr and Mrs Tanner, are in the back row.

A Corsham family produced as a postcard c.1912. They are sitting outside 19 Paul Street. Notice the iron railings (left) which were removed across the country as part of the war effort. It became common for families to have photographs made into postcards to send through the post to friends and relatives.

Victory in Europe celebrations in Erneston Crescent on Tuesday 8th May 1945. These fashionable semi-detached houses were built by, and named after the local builder Ernest Merrett at a cost of £350. A girl plays an accordion for the barn-dance circles.

The group assemble underneath the gas lamp-post which is decked out with home-made bunting, whilst their homes proudly display the Union Jack.

PICKWICK ROAD, WEST VIEW, CORSHAM

A postcard of Pickwick Road in 1907. This card was produced by Lewin Spackman at the Caxton Printing Works. It shows the large Victorian Houses built by the Head Brothers at the turn of the 20th Century. Their outlook at this time was fields (now houses). A female cyclist was something of a spectacle at the time!

The Neale and Gough brush factory in Pickwick Road. This rare photograph shows one of the employees assembling a hand-made brush. Mr Neale opened the factory in 1811. The factory was destroyed by fire on two separate occasions in 1888 and on the 24th May 1921.

Nurses' Home, Corsham.

The Nurses' Home, Corsham, on a postcard sent in 1917. This was important accommodation for the volunteer nurses who cared for wounded soldiers at the Red Cross (VAD) Hospital in the High Street. The hospital closed in 1919. Several nurses have gathered on the first floor balcony for this postcard. The house was built in 1909.

This postcard shows a group of nurses outside their Home in Pickwick Road in 1915. There is a senior sister and to her right, Lady Methuen. Photo by Herbert Spackman.

34

3. PICKWICK, HARTHAM and BIDDESTONE

This 1905 postcard claims that: 'This inn is famous as having been the residence of Moses Pickwick, founder of the celebrated Moses Pickwick Coaches, the stage from London to Bath. Dickens, in travelling by this route, became acquainted with the owner and gave his name to his famous work "Pickwick Papers".

The Hare and Hounds in 1906. The sign (right) reads: 'The Hare and Hounds Inn - Good Accommodation for Cyclists'. Notice the picket fence.

Pickwick, near Corsham.

This village gave the name to the famous "Pickwick Papers," by Dickens. A boy picked up here was named Moses Pickwick, becoming ostler and eventually landlord of the Hare and Hounds Inn, where the horses were changed in the old stage coach days. He became founder and owner of the celebrated Moses Pickwick Coaches from London to Bath. Dickens, in travelling by this route, being acquainted with the history of the owner and the place, adopted its name as the title for his famous work, introducing to his readers many of the characters found here. (See Post Card of "Hare and Hounds.")

A delightful view of the heart of Pickwick. The association of Pickwick with Dicken's 'Pickwick Papers' is provided on this postcard from 1911. The Ostler's house is the building on the right where Moses Pickwick changed the coach horses. The hooks for the PICKWICK sign (left) are still there!

Pickwick Street. Corsham

The Spread Eagle pub on a postcard of Pickwick posted in 1928. Corpses were literally 'spread eagled' on the bar before being taken to the mortuary in Corsham?! A horse-drawn delivery cart is delivering beer barrels from Ushers Brewery in Trowbridge .

The centre of Pickwick in the summer of 1907. This scene captures a lost world when the pace of life was much slower. The sign for the Spread Eagle pub is on the right. Several local boys have stopped playing to be frozen in time by the photographer. On the left is the stone tiled roof of the Masons' Hall. Published by R.F. Houlston of Chippenham.

The village of Pickwick on the A4 (Bath Road) in 1967. The Pickwick Stores is covered in the late afternoon sun. The Spread Eagle and Hare & Hounds public houses are here. The doorway on the far right was the entrance to the Masonic Hall and has a symbol carved by Mr Coles above the doorway.

The Hudswell cottages on the outskirts of the town (west) near Rudloe. These fine Corsham stone cottages with their stone-tiled roofs were probably built as servant's cottages and later for quarry workers. The small group of girls in the foreground adds to this idyllic picture which was discovered in New Zealand!

Pockeridge House at the end of Pockeridge Drive to the south west of Corsham. It was once owned by Mr. John Edridge, one of the original Christian Brethren who still meet at the Gospel Hall at Neston. This is now the Officers Mess, Basil Hill Barracks, Corsham. Notice the extensive ivy, croquet hoops and a sword!

In 1937 the government began the requisition of Corsham's underground quarries. The threat of a second major conflict in Europe required large bombproof storage and ammunition areas. The disused quarries in and around Corsham were perfect sites. These pictures show local labourers clearing out thousands of tons of debris prior to the development of the secret underground military network codenamed 'Burlington'.

An R.A.O.C (Royal Army Ordnance Corps - Southern Command) soldier supervises the conveyor belt in 'No.5' shaft at Basil Hill (Hawthorn). There were six such underground shafts. In 1943, 300,000 tons of high explosives were stored underground in disused quarries in and around Corsham. These caverns created during the stone mining played a vital part of the 1939-45 campaign.

An R.A.O.C soldier stacking "5.5's". These 5.5-inch medium field gun high explosives were stored underground in disused quarries during World War II. Each shell weighed 8lbs.

Sunset at Weavern near Corsham.

'Sunset at Weavern near Corsham'. This postcard, from June 1905 shows a valley waterway (Bybrook) which is a tributary of the River Avon. Herbert Spackman informs us in his diary that this beauty spot was a favourite swimming and picnic area for the residents of Corsham, Pickwick and nearby Box.

Pickwick House in 1931. This fine Victorian residence was the home of the Pictor family. When Mrs Pictor died, the house was left to the eldest son who owned one of the stone quarries. Miss Joan Pictor bought Arnold House in the High Street, which she bequeathed to the Town Council. Photograph by Herbert Spackman.

Beechfield House in Pickwick (1915). This was the home of Sir Frederick Goldney (1845-1940). The formal entrance had a tree-lined avenue. Corsham has a number of large houses including Neston Park, Hartham House, Middlewick House and Corsham Court. The house was used by Bath Academy of Art in the 1960's and 70's. It was recently renovated into exclusive flats.

Beechfield House in 1909. This fine Georgian residence was the home of Sir Frederick Goldney (1845-1940). His wife, Lady Goldney, was an inspiration to the work of the Red Cross Hospital (Town Hall) during the Great War 1914-18.

Middlewick House (1907) is a fine Georgian residence at the end of Middlewick Lane. The lawn is prepared for tennis (right edge shows net). This was the residence of Camilla Parker Bowles (The Duchess of Cornwall), who describing Corsham said: *"It's such a friendly place and still has a lot of charm about it."*

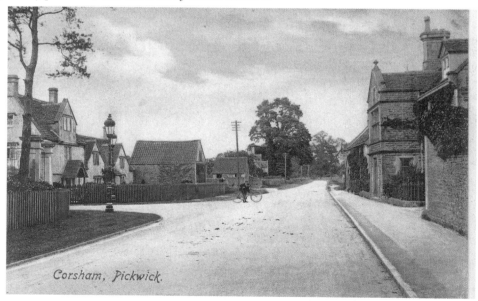

Pickwick in 1907. This postcard shows the ornate main entrance lamps to Beechfield House drive (left). Mead Cottage (left) dates from the 17th century. Sperring's Garage is also shown. There is a sign for the Pickwick Dairy. When this postcard was sent there was no right turn into Priory Street.

Corsham, Beechfield Gates.

Beechfield Gates was the official entrance, off the Bath Road (A4), into Beechfield House. The wrought iron gates (left) led to a tree-lined avenue to the main house. These beautiful 17th century cottages with mullion windows and stone-tiled roofing still exist. The card was posted from Corsham in 1905 and includes this message: *"Dear Gerty, this is granny's house where we are staying."*

BATH ROAD, (NEAR HARTHAM LANE) CORSHAM.

The Bath Road (A4), at the junction of Hartham Lane (left) mid-way between the Cross Keys and the village of Pickwick. This photo was published by Lewin Spackman at the Caxton Printing Works. Just in sight is an approaching traction engine!

HARTHAM CHURCH.

PUBLISHED BY ARTHUR LITTLE, HIGH STREET, CORSHAM.

Hartham Church on the Hartham Estate. The photograph was taken by Herbert Spackman for Arthur Little who ran a shop in Pickwick Road. This private chapel was built in 1862 in the perpendicular style to a design by P.C. Hardwick. Sir John and Lady Dickson-Poynder owned the Hartham Estate in 1909.

Hartham House in 1931. In 1846, Hartham Park, with 77 acres of land, was leased to John Ashton Case for £330 per annum. Stables were added in 1858. It was home to Sir John Dickson-Poynder, later Lord Islington who was Governor of New Zealand. The garden was designed by H.A. Peto. Extensive climbing ivy is indicative of the period.

HARTHAM HOUSE.   The Tennis Court.   Tomkins & Barrett, Swindon

The famous Sticke indoor tennis court at Hartham House in 1906. This wooden framed building was constructed for Sir John Dickson-Poynder (Lord Islington) in 1904. The game of Sticke Tennis was named after its inventor, Major-General Sticke. It was a combination of Lawn Tennis with a net, and squash. It is one of the only surviving examples in the world.

The Dutch Garden in the grounds of Hartham House (1910). Notice the stone tiled gazebo. The garden is neatly laid out for Lady Dickson-Poynder to enjoy. The estate gardens were landscaped by Harold Peto of Iford Manor.

Sir J. D. Poynder.   Tomkins and Barrett, Swindon.

Studio photograph of Sir John Dickson-Poynder (1866–1936), 17th Governor of New Zealand. Born Ryde, I.O.W., the only son of Rear-Admiral J. B. Dickson. Educated at Harrow and Oxford. In 1888 'J.D.P.' assumed the additional surname of Poynder. He represented North-west Wiltshire (1892–1910), as a Conservative and later as a Liberal. He served as A.D.C. to Lord Methuen in the Boer War. Awarded D.S.O.

Lady Dickson Poynder   Tomkins & Barrett, Swindon.

This is an interesting postcard made from a portrait of Lady Dickson-Poynder. The picture hung inside Hartham House mansion at the turn of the 20th century when it was home to Sir John Dickson-Poynder. The postcard was posted from Chippenham in February 1905. Their daughter adds innocence to this portrait postcard.

To view the whole collection or to purchase additional copies of this and other books online visit:
www.corshampostcards.com

Marsh Son & Gibbs Ltd, mined stone in the Hartham Quarry from 1905. It was later worked by the Yockney and Hartham Park Stone Company. A horse is pulling a block of stone out of the quarry along a rail track. The large stack of sawn stone is arranged in such a way as to allow free passage of summer air to facilitate 'drying out'.

A calling card for Copenacre Ground Stone. The Yockney and Hartham Park Stone Company. This is the Art Gallery in Bristol which was constructed from Corsham quarried stone. A company stamp has been impressed into the postcard (top right). Many of the exterior and internal carvings were carved by banker masons in Corsham.

The summer stacking yard at the Hartham Park underground stone quarry. In 1840, when Brunel decided to tunnel from Corsham to Box, huge quantities of oolite limestone were discovered. The result was a successful stone industry in the town which continues today. This picture shows thousands of cubic feet of stone blocks stacked to dry and harden. Each block was individually numbered before transportation.

Southwark Cathedral on an advertising postcard for Bath Stone supplied by Yockney and Hartham Company. Thousands of cubic feet of stone were literally sawn from underground quarries and then transported from Corsham Railway Station.

Biddestone Church on a postcard sent from Corsham in 1905. The nave and chancel of St. Nicholas are Norman. Carvings of the period can still be seen around the south door. The bell-turret was added in the 13th century. A sanctuary and vestry were added in the 19th century. The churchyard includes an interesting array of gravestones and box tombs.

The Rectory at Biddestone. This postcard dates from c.1910. This building was constructed before 1830. It is found at the end of a beautiful avenue of lime trees and lies directly opposite the church of St. Nicholas on Church Road.

50

The outskirts of Biddestone in 1911. This is the fork to Slaughterford and Yatton Keynell. It was taken by the photographer C. Young. Two girls pose for the camera wearing smock dresses. A poster behind them reads 'Chippenham Order 1907' which accurately dates this simple rural scene.

Mr. C. Young of Teddington, entered Biddestone in 1909 and took at least seven pictures of the village. This shows the duck pond and the open expanse of the village green looking east. The large flagstones are believed to be all that remains of a medieval ducking stool in the days when witches and others were 'tried'. The house on the right is part of Pool Farm.

Women gather at the village pump on this postcard of Biddestone from 1910. The back of Elm Lodge, built in 1878, is on the right. Notice the road surface and horse debris on Church Road looking towards the village green. Mr C. Young took the photograph in 1909. In the centre (distance) is Elm Farm and Home Place built in the 17th century.

Church Road, Biddestone on a postcard from 1906. The Well Head pump, now disused, was an essential reservoir and meeting point. It stands next to Turnpike Cottages. The circular stone-tiled roof was added in 1901. A delivery cart is off-loading flour to the old bakehouse. This road leads towards an area known as The Butts and the route to Corsham via Hartham.

CONSECRATION OF BIDDESTONE BURIAL GROUND, JUNE 28, 1915.
(SPACKMAN.)

This Herbert Spackman photographic postcard records the Consecration of Biddestone Burial Ground on June 28th 1915. The Bishop of Bristol (Rt. Rev. George Nickson) is led into the cemetery by two churchwardens carrying staves. The whole village has turned out for this important event.

Biddestone

Elm Cottage on the western edge of the village pond. This thatched cottage was built in the middle of the 17th century. The large, imposing oak, obscures the view eastward towards the village green. In the centre is the White Hart Inn.

This postcard was sent from Yatton Keynell in 1909. The boys are wearing plus fours and girls in white smock dresses. Left is the village shop run by H. White. Willow House, is the large, 3 storey house (centre). It was built of Bath Stone in 1760 for Samuel Alborne, his wife and their nine children. The photo is by T. A. Trotman of Chippenham.

This postcard is entitled 'Meet of Duke of Beaufort's Hounds at Biddestone, March 1907.' The Beaufort estate at Badminton has kept hounds since 1640. The 9th Duke turned to fox hunting in the mid 1700's. The hunt dress is peculiar in that the Huntsman and Whippers-In wear green and the subscribers a blue coat with buff facings. View from green west towards Biddestone Pond.

A fancy dress group gather in front of Willow House, Biddestone on August 28th 1920. This was taken by Herbert Spackman. None of these people have been identified by name. The youngest, if alive, would be over 90 years old now!

This captures the tranquillity of this perfect village scene. A horse-trap leaves the village on its way to Corsham. Closer inspection reveals a boy tucked away in the long grass. (centre right). The White Hart (left) has a long tradition of serving locals and travellers. Posted from Marshfield 1905.

The whole of Biddestone have gathered for the dedication of the Cross, May 22nd 1920. This event was recorded by the photographer Herbert Spackman, This monument was erected shortly after the end of the Great War of 1914-1918. The cottages in this area date back to the 17th century.

The thatched cottage, centre, was once the village Reading Room. It has been redesigned with a tiled roof and gabled windows. The Biddestone Arms is in this area of the village. A group of nine children have gathered and have been immortalised in this 1907 photographic postcard.

4. TO CORSHAM COURT

Priory Street in 1919. The Victorian cottages and walls are all built from locally quarried stone. The road declines gradually towards the northern end of the High Street. In the 19th century, Priory Street was known as Stumps Lane after a local wool merchant.

Priory Street Baptist Church in 1923. Lillian Selman (later Mrs Holder) presents Mrs Kinnear with a bouquet of flowers. The porch was built to commemorate 100 years of the Baptist movement in the town. Ernest Merrett, Kenneth Davis, Pastor Smith, Mrs Caleb Davis, Cecil Selman, Bert Brown and Mr Carter are among those gathered.

Ashford cottages on a photograph postcard dated c.1905. These cottages were named after the 4th Lord, Paul Ayshford Methuen (1886-1974). They were probably built for workers on the Methuen Estate. 'Big Jim' Smith was born in Priory Street and was one of two Corsham men to play professional cricket for England. The other was S.P. Kinneir.

PRIORY STREET, CORSHAM

The Duke of Cumberland public house (left) and the Ashford Cottages in Priory Street. This postcard was sold from J. Hunter's shop in the High Street. It dates from about 1911. The 'Duke' is reputed to be the oldest pub in Wiltshire.

58

The Priory in 1900, now Heywood House. The gentleman may be Capt. C.M. Leatham and his wife. Notice the gardener. Benedictine monks from Marmoutier Les Tours had an abbey cell here in the time of Henry I (1336) and this is mentioned in the Domesday Book. This Georgian edifice was constructed in 1776 from locally quarried stone. In 1904 an outbuilding housed the town's first horse-drawn fire engine.

Church Street, Corsham

Valentines Series 41665

Church Street in 1907. This narrow road connects the High Street with Church Square and St Bartholomew's Church. The wool trade prospered in the town during the 17th century and the white stone cottages in this street show many signs of this period of Corsham's history.

Corsham Church Street.

Church Street in 1907. The lamp mounted gates open into Church Square. Just visible in the distance (facing) is the Pack Horse pub in the High Street. Ethelred House (no.6) (right), is one of the large town houses. It is named after King Ethelred the Unready who had a 'Palace' in Corsham in 1015 and hunted in nearby Melksham forest.

A photograph of Corsham church prior to its restoration in 1874. The tower was completely removed, as it was unsafe. A new tower and spire were constructed near the south door. The clock at this time was square. A dormer window balcony to the nave (centre), built for the Hungerford family, was also removed.

St. Bartholomew's Church from the park in 1904. A lone figure admires this quintessential English country church. The tower and spire were rebuilt in the 19th century and contain six bells. The church contains a memorial to Alice Cobb, who having given birth to thirteen children lived to bury all but three.

A wedding at St. Bartholomew's Parish Church, This postcard photograph from the late 1920's shows the bride and groom passing through the assembled guests. Rice, rather than confetti, is being thrown for good luck. If you know who the happy couple are, visit www.corshampostcards.com

The interior of the Parish Church of St Bartholomew. It shows a harvest festival in 1906. The pulpit (right) was moved to this position in 1850. The nave looks through to the Chancel eastwards. The Chancel was an addition and is at an angle to the nave. The Eagle lectern (centre left) is the king of birds 'carrying The Word on its back'.

Clergy, Choir and Church Wardens on a postcard photograph by Herbert Spackman (1912). Two of the clergy wear preaching scarves. The organist (Lewin Spackman) is seated far right. Mr Mallard is standing (far left). This was taken outside the vestry door.

Herbert Spackman's camera records a visit from the Bishop of Bristol. The choir process behind the wooden cross towards a chair for the Bishop. The musicians (right) included Herbert Spackman who was probably the lead violinist! Lewin Spackman (organist for 50 years) is on the extreme left. The building is the Riding School at Corsham Court.

Entrance to Corsham Court.

The entrance to Corsham Court on a postcard sent from Corsham in 1905. The South front of the house was built by 'Customer' Smythe during the reign of Elizabeth I. It is one of the country's finest examples of Elizabethan architecture. The Estate has remained in the hands of the Methuen family since 1745.

Corsham Chnrch & Avenue, from Court.   *Photo by Herbert Spackman.*

Corsham Parish Church of St Bartholomew and the South Avenue and Park. Taken from an upper room of Corsham Court by Herbert Spackman. Can you see the peacock? Sold from James Barnes shop in Pickwick road in 1909.

The Elizabethan south face of Corsham Court in 1907. It shows the Methuen coat of arms and motto: 'Virtus Invidiae Scopus'. In the centre is a Judas tree. The Court has been in the Methuen family since 1745 and is famous for the Picture Gallery designed by 'Capability' Brown in the 1760's.

The Picture Gallery in 1907. It is extremely unlikely that plants were ever kept in this centrepiece of the Methuen art collection. The triple-cube room is 72ft by 24 ft. It contains works by masters including, Carlo Dolci, Van Dyck, Bernardo Strozzi and Rubens. The ornate ceiling is a work of art itself.

65

Corsham House on a print dated October 1st 1813. The artist was Thompson. In 1813 the House was the residence of Paul Cobb Methuen (1752-1816). Nash's Gothic design (1803) was ornate but proved inadequate accommodation for the Methuen art collection. It lasted only 50 years and was pulled down and replaced.

The north face of Corsham Court on a 1904 postcard. It was designed by Thomas Bellamy between 1846 and 1849. This replaced the remodelling by John Nash (above).

Corsham Court (West Side).

The west wing of the Court in 1915. John Nash remodelled parts of the house which included castellations to this part of the house. These castle-like additions included octagonal turrets to three corners. The yew hedge (left) was planted in 1845 and lines the trade entrance to the estate buildings. The south-facing kitchens and servants-quarters (centre) included shutters to block out the afternoon sunlight.

Corsham Court, Yew Hedge

The Yew hedge on the western extremity of Corsham Court. This perfectly kept topiary hedge lines a trade entrance to the estate from the top of the high street near the Flemish Houses. Gardens in this area are of historic interest. The first Lady Methuen was responsible for the layout of many of the flower gardens.

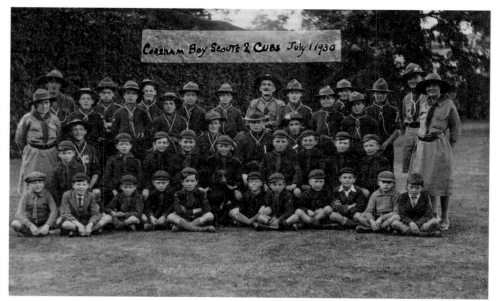

Corsham Boy Scouts and Cubs with their leaders in July 1930. Scouting began in Corsham in 1908. The Methuens encouraged and supported the movement from its beginning. This photograph, by Herbert Spackman, was taken on the western lawn of Corsham Court; the yew hedge can be seen. None of these people have been identified. The youngest would now be aged about 90!

A summer production in the grounds of Corsham Court c.1920. A large group have gathered to view the pageant. In the background is the topiary hedge which lines the western trade entrance. This postcard was produced by Herbert Spackman.

The noblest spur unto the sons of fame,
Is thirst of honour. John Hall.

With love & best wishes
from George & Charlie
Xmas 1903.

Lord Methuen and his Staff.

A beautiful, colour-embossed postcard of General Lord Methuen (1845-1932) entitled 'Lord Methuen and his Staff'. Paul Sanford Methuen was the third peer and lived at Corsham Court, which he inherited in 1891. He served in the Scots Fusilier Guards in 1864. He was appointed General in 1904. He was made commander in Chief in South Africa between 1908-12 and was appointed Field Marshal in 1911.

LT.-GEN. LORD METHUEN

Studio photograph of Lord Methuen (1845-1932) of Corsham Court. He was promoted to Lieut. General in 1898. He was appointed to command the 1st Division on the outbreak of the Boer war in South Africa in 1899. He is wearing the band of the Scots Guards, which he joined in 1864 at the age of 19 and became their Colonel in 1904 and General at the same time. He became Field Marshal in 1911 and Governor of Malta in 1915.

Corsham Park and lake on the Estate. In 1760 'Capability' Brown was entrusted with the work of enlarging the Park and house. He included a 13-acre lake, which was completed by Humphry Repton. This area has been used as grazing land for centuries and the people of Corsham continue to enjoy this landscaped beauty spot to the present day.

Corsham Park in 1907 looking east. This postcard includes a twisted lightning tree. Corsham lake is just visible in the distance.

The Lake, Corsham Park

Valentines Series 41668

Repton built this 13-acre Lake c.1800. This postcard was sent from Corsham in 1909. In 1800, John Nash was commissioned to enlarge Corsham House. At the turn of the century successive 'hard' winters froze the lake and hundreds of people would come from as far as Bath and Bristol to enjoy this natural ice rink!

The "Eel Pond" Corsham Lake

The Lake and Boating House. This postcard is entitled 'The Eel Pond'. The boathouse was constructed by John Nash to create a focal point from the gallery of the Court. This was sent by the photographer W.R.H. Ray in 1906 to Fred Bryant who ran the Post Office in the High Street.

AVENUE FROM CHURCH SQUARE, CORSHAM.

The South Avenue of Elm trees extend from the main entrance of Corsham Court to South Place. 'Capability' Brown planted this avenue in 1760 to give the impression that the Court was surrounded by countryside and in so doing obscured the backs of town houses and shops.

The South Avenue from the south gates (South Place) looking towards the main entrance of Corsham Court. This avenue was laid out in 1760 to give the impression that Corsham Court estate was surrounded by countryside. These original trees were lost to Dutch Elm disease in the mid 1970s.

The south gates at the entrance to the South Avenue leading to Corsham Court. The Victorian lodge is on the left. These are the original wrought iron gates which were cast by Stothert and Pitt of Bath. They were removed around 1940 to assist with the war effort. The avenue was part of the landscaping design of Lancelot (Capability) Brown.

Delightful, hand-tinted colour postcard of South Place. These imposing gates were erected around 1720 when 'Capability' Brown was making extensive changes to Corsham Court and the Park. The Lodge (centre) is Victorian; above the east window are the 3 wolves which form part of the Methuen family crest. These also appear on the gates themselves which lead to a long elm tree avenue to the Court.

This postcard, called 'Corsham Contingent for the War' was taken by Herbert Spackman on September 27th 1914. It includes soldiers from the Somerset Light Infantry, a sailor and one older soldier (back row, 6th from left) wearing a long service medal from the

Field Marshal Lord Methuen watches as Lady Methuen unveils the War Memorial. A large crowd gathered on this wet June morning in 1920. Amongst them, Charlie Bethel, the last Corsham Town Cryer (behind Lord Methuen).

5. The Road to Lacock and Gastard

THE ALMSHOUSES, CORSHAM.
Built by Lady Hungerford, 1672. One of the finest examples of the post-Reformation Almshouse.

A beautiful watercolour of the Almshouses and Warden's house by Walter Tyndale (1856-1943). It states that it was 'Built by Lady Hungerford 1672. One of the finest examples of the post reformation Almshouse.' The picture, painted in 1906, shows the Warden talking to two small girls, one with a hoop. The Warden has a wooden leg and a stick; some degree of artist licence used here!

The Almshouses is one of the town's most photographed images and the subject of many postcards. The building was completed in 1668 by Dame Margaret Hungerford to accommodate six poor people. Above the main entrance is the Hungerford Coat of Arms.

Corsham, Warden's House.

A hand-coloured postcard of the entrance to the Corsham Almshouses and Warden's house in 1925. The inhabitants had to be God-fearing, go to church regularly and attend prayers twice a day. Notice the fine lime trees and topiary peacock which were removed around 1960.

76

Extremely rare photographic postcard showing the back of the Almshouses looking northwest. On the left are the arched windows of the 17th century schoolroom. This 1906 postcard shows the intimate accommodation built for 6 poor people of the parish. On the ground level are the cloisters. The grass has been recently scythed.

The Chapel and Schoolroom in the Almshouses. The balcony is finely carved with aspects from the Hungerford Coat of Arms. It founder, Dame Margaret Hungerford, would have easily recognised this scene which has remained largely unchanged for over 250 years.

Lacock Road on a postcard sent from Corsham in May 1905. The wall (right) is the boundary to Corsham Park on the Corsham Estate. The Almshouses are just visible in the distance. The vicarage on the left was built in 1904 because the vicar's wife did not agree with living in the High Street opposite a butcher's shop! There were complaints at the time because it was not built of local stone; the result of a clerical error!

Westrop Lodge situated on the eastern edge of the Corsham Estate at the junction of Lacock Road and Westrop Road. Two characters sit chatting, but who are they? One has a sea captain's cap and the other looks decidedly Scottish and has a long white beard!

CONSECRATION OF NEW BURIAL GROUND, CORSHAM, OCT. 14. 1911.
ARRIVAL OF BISHOP OF BRISTOL.

The Bishop of Bristol exits the carriage for the consecration of the burial ground in Ladbrook Lane. This superb photograph postcard was taken by Herbert Spackman on October 14th 1911. A large crowd have gathered for this important opening. The Bishop wears a 'Canterbury Cap'. Churchwardens from the Parish Church of St. Bartholomew's escort him with their ceremonial staves.

CHURCH BURYING GROUND, CORSHAM

A postcard from 1913 entitled 'Church Burying Ground'. There are only seven graves visible in this picture. This postcard was produced by Lewin Spackman from the Caxton Printing Works. The small chapel was designed by William Osborne who was later buried here.

The Methuen School c.1905. The Methuen School was founded in 1816. These students were educated free of charge. They had one teacher and two classrooms. Floors were part stone and part wooden. The teacher is Miss Freeth. In 1923, the mixed infants were taught at this school and older children at the nearby County Junior School. Can anyone help identify any of these children?

The Methuen School is situated in South Place. This photographic postcard shows 'Class I'. On the back is written *'Joan Fortune, Paul St. Corsham'*. Joan and Joyce Mallard twins are also here (left). Can anyone help identify any of the others?

Two gents stand casually in the late afternoon sun in front of the Almshouses and Warden's house in 1909. This Corsham landmark was completed in 1668 for six poor people. Above the entrance porch is the Hungerford Coat of Arms after its founder, Dame Margaret Hungerford, who established 45 orders for its government.

The Almshouses on the approach to Corsham from the south in 1906. In the distance is South Place with the lodge, pillars and gates to the south carriage drive to Corsham Court. The gate, right, leads into the Almshouse gardens and an area originally used for stabling. On the left is the boundary wall of Corsham cricket field established in 1847.

81

Group of army soldier cadets on November 11th, 1930. Several have bugles. The drum has the Wiltshire White Horse emblem. The Corsham Park is behind. Among them are Frank Dyke, Bond, Vowells, Holder, Cyril Fido, Eric Harris, Angel.

Corsham Band was established in 1888. This picture from 1949 was taken after the band had won the Chippenham Carnival contest. Pictured here (sitting L-R): Tony Pike, Jean North, Jack Cramp (band master), David Williams, Cecil Smith. (Standing L-R): Ernie Foot, Arthur Hulbert, ?, Alf Hazlewood, ?, John Salter, Peter Hulbert, ?, ?, Peter Gale, Bill Philpotts, Alf Rawlings, Jack Hayward, ?

Ash Villa on Pound Pill c.1905. This view shows the monkey-puzzle tree on the south facing lawn. Notice the lawn mower (right). In 1830 this was home to Uriah Goold who established a nearby Tanyard and was also a founder member of the Baptist Church in Priory Street. Daisy Goold married the photographer, Herbert Spackman, who was probably responsible for this photograph.

Group of local 'lads' outside Altus Engineering Company in Stokes Road. Identified (left to right) as Ian (Jock) Wiseman, Sid Mason, Harry Pritchard (one time goalkeeper for Corsham Town F.C.), Les Simkins, ?, Ken Coleman, Jack Macmillan and Eric Mallows.

Pound Pill in 1912. The Great Western Inn derives its name from its proximity to the railway line from London to Bristol and the famous Box Tunnel engineered by Isambard Kingdom Brunel. The incline leads to the nearby village of Gastard. To the left is the entrance to the tanyard and stone quarry.

Pound Pill and Railway Bridge c.1908. The bridge was widened in the 1950's as the use of the motorcar increased. The County School is in the distance (far left) with the Corsham Park in the distance. The area bottom right leads to an area known locally as The Batters.

84

Corsham Trenches (9) Spackman.

Scots Guards on 'shirt sleeve order' in The Batters. These soldiers used a piece of land on the south of the railway for trench practice before going to 'The Front'.

Herbert Spackman, Corsham's local photographer, took at least ten of this spectacle. How many of these young men saw action and were killed in France?

The Batters area of Corsham still shows the undulations made by these soldiers in 1915.

To view the whole collection or to purchase additional copies of this and other books online visit
 www.corshampostcards.com

Scots Guards in Trenches, Corsham Batters. (Spackman)

Claremont is situated in an area of the town known as Broadstone near the hamlet of the Linleys. This was probably built as a private house c.1840. In 1910 it was a girls' private college run by Misses Tennant and Rigden. Observe the croquet hoops and bicycle. Walled ivy was common at this time. The card mentions a prize giving and D.M.M. who was doubtless one of the pupils.

The Linleys is a tiny hamlet between Corsham and the village of Gastard. The road narrows here and creates a natural chicane for today's busy traffic! At this time these stone tiled cottages, with their thick walls were only disturbed by the occasional sound of horse hooves.

This is Monks Park near Neston. It is an ancient estate comprising the Monks, Boys, Goods, and Snippets. In 1357 Monks belonged to a family of that name and later Thomas Tropenell, of Neston, in 1463. This fine mansion was erected by the Dickinsons' about 1780. It was home to Sir Gabriel Goldney MP for Chippenham until 1885.

Monks Chapel was built by the Quakers in 1662. This ancient non-conformist chapel is still a place of Christian worship today. It was built on land belonging to Mr Monk. It appears as a cottage at a time, when non-established worship was illegal!

Sawing out Stone from the Rock in the Monks Park Mine.

Two 'sawyers' cutting out stone from Monks Park mine. This was slow and backbreaking work. Pay was at half-a-crown per square yard. Monks Park quarry, also known as Sumsion's Monks began life in 1886. The stone from this quarry was very hard with a fine grain. The quarry was prone to flooding. The 'ganger' in charge was H. Hancock.

The Stone Quarries. Corsham.
These Quarries are very extensive.
The Galleries are from 20 to 50
feet in height, and blocks of stone
containing 200 cubic feet are some-
times raised to the surface.

A stack of dried Monks Park stone. This stone was perfect for working by banker masons. Brunel's excavation of Box Tunnel in 1840 revealed valuable seams of oolite limestone and the result was a profitable local industry. Large areas were developed underground. One cavern is known as 'The Cathedral' because of its size.

MONKS PARK STONE

A VERY RELIABLE AND ECONOMICAL BUILDING STONE, CLOSE IN GRAIN AND EVEN IN TEXTURE.

LARGE STOCKS AVAILABLE FOR IMMEDIATE DESPATCH.

ENQUIRIES INVITED AND ESTIMATES WILLINGLY GIVEN.

THE BATH & PORTLAND STONE FIRMS LTD.

LONDON.	BATH.	MANCHESTER.
47 Victoria St.	Tel: 3248-9	Grosvenor Chambers,
S.W.1.		16 Deansgate,
Tel: Franklin 6636.		Tel: Blackfriars 4922.

This is the reverse of the postcard below for The Bath and Portland Stone Firms Ltd. The company was established in 1887. It promotes Monks Park stone, which has the finest grain and was considered by quarrymen and builders to be the highest quality stone of any of the quarries in the Corsham area. The quarry opened in 1886.

Homeopathic Hospital, Bristol.   ARTS: OATLEY & LAWRENCE, F.F.R.I.B.A.

"MONKS PARK" STONE.

The Homeopathic Hospital Bristol on an advertising postcard. This building was constructed in 1921 using 'Monks Park Stone' hewn from an underground quarry situated 1.5 miles south east of Corsham. The hospital was designed by George Oatley.

89

The procession of clergy enters Gastard for the laying of the foundation stone of Gastard Church on July 11th, 1912. Gastard folk line the route. Herbert Spackman recorded this event for posterity. Amongst the company were members of his own family including the organist Lewin Spackman. Notice the builder's rubble (right).

Herbert Spackman set up his camera tripod and recorded the procession from St. Bartholomew's Parish church to Gastard. This was for the dedication of Gastard Church on June 24th 1913. These are the original Stothert and Pitt iron gates to the South Avenue of Corsham Court. Notice the absence of the war memorial (erected in 1920) right.

The procession of clergy and choirboys enters Gastard from Coppershell for the dedication of the church in 1913. The processional cross leads the company. On the roadside are the people of Gastard in their Sunday best. Herbert Spackman, Corsham's local photographer, recorded this event from start to finish. Amongst the company were members of his family including the organist Lewin Spackman.

Gastard village church was dedicated June 24th 1913. The laying of the foundation stone took place on July 11th 1912. This photograph by Herbert Spackman from Lanes End, records the completed church following its dedication in 1913. The Harp and Crown pub is in the distance. Postally used, July 1913.

Christmas Greetings
from GASTARD

FOND WISHES

I wish you joy,
I wish you well,
Far more than these
few words can tell.

A beautiful Edwardian postcard offering 'Christmas Greetings from Gastard.' This village is situated approximately 2 miles south east of Corsham. The postcard was posted from Gastard in December 1908. It was sent by Maud to Mr and Mrs George and Annie Freegard, Monks Cottage near Corsham. Greeting cards such as this one were mass produced and then different place names added. In 1908, the population of the village was less than 500 residents.

Mr Dent and Gastard School boys, June 24th 1913. This photographic postcard was taken by Herbert Spackman. Sadly, none of these Gastard children have been identified.

Chapel Knapp A.F.C. 1926-7. This football team played for a small hamlet of houses at the top of Velley Hill near Gastard, Corsham. On the front row (far left) is "Titch" Gale. Reginald Gale (known as Gank), is 2nd from left. Reg was 17 years old. None of the others have yet been identified. Can you help? If so, visit www.corshampostcards.com

This fine mansion is situated at the top of Velley Hill in Chapel Knap near Gastard about 2.5 miles south east of Corsham. It was posted from Neston in April 1905. This view shows the south and east face of Elm House. The tower is a notable landmark. It was the home of Captain Sir Thomas Fowler, who was an officer in the Imperial Yeomanry and was killed on 20 April 1902, in the Boer War. John Fowler (b.1826-1864), invented the steam plough.

6. To The Railway Station

H.Banks carriage business at the top of Station Hill. The business sign advertises 'Open and Close Carriages'. The Methuen Arms Hotel is in the distance. Mr Banks is the gentleman in the foreground with a dog. Photo by Herbert Spackman c.1902.

The Almshouses from Cricket Field, Corsham   Valentines Series   41670

'Sheep may safely graze' on Corsham's cricket ground in 1906. Cricket has been played here since 1847. The club was formed by Frederick, 2nd Baron Methuen. This card shows the Almshouses (right) and the pillars of the south gates entrance to the court.

The Lyndhurst 'Dame' School in Grove Road, 1925. These private day schools were popular at the time. The teacher is Mrs Head. Front row left to right: Margaret Kennedy, Marjorie Davis, unknown, Clarice Carter, Jack Lawerence, Dennis? Behind the teacher are Kenneth Pearce and Dick Riddle (sitting on the wall).

This is 24 Hastings Road which was built by the stonemason Nathaniel Fido for his family. On the picture is Alice (b.1885) aged 20 and Lily Fido (b.1890) aged 15. The postcard was sent by Nathaniel's daughter Alice (b.1885) to her uncle, Charles Fido of Goblins Pit Corsham Side (Neston). It was sent from Corsham on July 22nd 1905. The railings were removed 9 years later because of WWI.

GARDEN OF REMEMBRANCE, CORSHAM

The Garden of Remembrance at the corner of Station Road and Stokes Road. This war memorial was unveiled by Lieut. Philip Mountbatten shortly after his engagement to Princess Elizabeth (Queen Elizabeth II) in 1947. Large crowds gathered including many from HMS Royal Arthur Corsham where the Prince was stationed. The postcard was sent from Corsham in 1953. The house behind the memorial is 38 Station Road built in 1893.

The Second World War Memorial was given to the parish by Misses Tennant and Rigden. This picture shows a youthful Lieut. Philip Mountbatten addressing the assembled crowd on November 1st 1947. This was the Queen's future husband's first post-engagement address. Representatives from each of the armed forces gathered at this solemn occasion which was recorded by the Gaumont British Newsreel cameras.

To view the whole collection or to purchase additional copies of this and other books online visit:
www.corshampostcards.com

Graham Olds Butchers Corsham is on a tiny sign underneath the crossbar of the bicycle. This was the only clue to identify the card. Research has discovered more: Graham Olds is on the far right. Jimmy Waite, aged 19, is in the centre. The business was at the back of the Railway Station Hotel, later used by Hancocks to store coal. Notice the raw meat being hung out and the Harris' of Calne posters.

GRAHAM OLDS

Butcher   Butcher

STATION RD., CORSHAM

1925 advert for Graham Olds Butcher.

1909 view of the Station booking office and station hotel. This card was sold by W. Field from his shop in the High Street. Everything here has been demolished and this is an excellent pictorial reminder. At one stage the Station Hotel was operated by Dan Tasker.

A superb postcard of the booking office and waiting room at the railway station. B. Davis posted it from Neston post office in January 1903. It shows Mr H. Banks driving one of his horse carriages. Banks transported passengers to and from the station. His business was situated at the top of Station Road next to the cricket field. Notice the G.W.R. posters and local lads in plus fours. In later life, Banks became manager of the Royal Wilts Butchers shop in the High Street.

The old railway station platform at the height of its popularity before the closure by Beeching in the 1960s. The only aspect which remains is the footbridge; everything else has gone. Will it ever look like this again? GWR posters are visible against the waiting room in this fine postcard from the turn of the 20th Century.

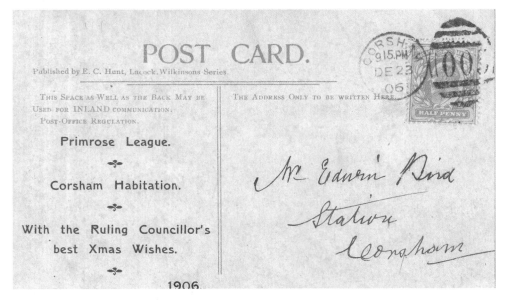

This postcard was sent from the Primrose League in Corsham at Christmas to Mr Edwin Bird, Station Corsham in 1906. Mr Bird is assumed to have be the stationmaster at the railway station. The primrose league was a political organisation formed in 1883 to spread Conservative principles. Sir H. D. Wolff suggested the idea to Lord Randolph Churchill. The primrose was Lord Beaconsfield's favourite flower.

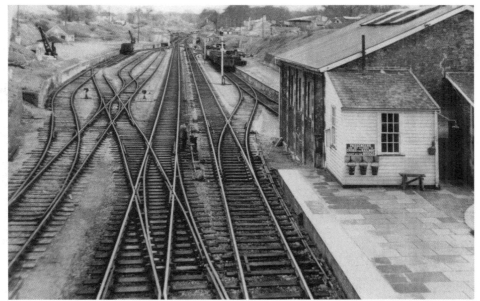

Photograph of Corsham Railway Station looking west (upline) around 1950. The station shed is on the right. Notice the three sand buckets and a sign warning passengers to use the footbridge from where this picture was taken. There is obvious activity at the wharf with trucks and several quarry stone cranes on the wharf (left). A man is checking the points.

This is Corsham Station looking west (upline) around 1950. The station shed is on the right. This was taken from the station platform. Notice the footbridge (top) which is all that remains following the Beeching reorganisation and closure of 1965.

View of the railway station from The Cleeve. This postcard was sold by F.W. Reeves in 1928. The Station Hotel and pedestrian iron bridge are in the centre. The land in the foreground is now Telcroft Close. This view also shows South Street, Hastings Road, Station Hill and the County School in Pound Pill.

(left) James and Maria Jane Jeffery, the local School's attendance officer, outside their home in The Cleeve. This photograph was taken on the marriage of their daughter Ethel Jeffery to Henry Thomas Clark on Tuesday, June 6th 1911. The best man was Frederick Clark and the bridesmaids were Hilda and Mabel Jeffery. Corsham's population (census year 1911) was 4,209. The king was George V and Asquith was Prime Minister.

102

Travelling Post Office at Corsham. This was the way to travel! The train is leaving Corsham on its way to London via Chippenham. The railwayman loaded the postbag and the train literally 'snatched' it without stopping. Posted from Yatton Keynell post office at 9 p.m.!

Unique postcard sent by M. Aust from Corsham in 1905. It shows the 'snatcher' and a postman. This simple mechanical device allowed for the passing train to literally snatch the local postbag as it passed through without the need to stop. It was situated east of the railway bridge in Ladbrook Lane about a mile and a half from Corsham Station.

Superb photograph c.1880 showing railway engineers at the Corsham entrance to Box Tunnel. Work on Brunel's great project commenced in September 1836 and the tunnel was opened on 23rd June 1841. Notice the narrow gauge track, a smaller tunnel (known as no. 7) right leading to underground stone quarries and steps to ground level.

We are obliged for your order which is having our attention.
Yours faithfully, YOCKNEY & Co.

Advertising postcard c.1908 for Yockney and Co. Started by Marsh Son & Gibbs in 1905, it became the Yockney and Hartham Park Stone Company. Carefully numbered blocks of 'Bath Stone' can be seen entering a smaller tunnel called Number 7 leading to Tunnel Quarry. Box Tunnel was completed in 1841 at a cost of over £500,000.

104

7. The Road to Neston

This is one of three postcards produced in 1908 for Jack Swain who ran Neston Post Office in Elley Green. Neston is comprised of a number of smaller hamlets including Corshamside, Lock's Cross, Moor Green, Elley Green, Baker's Corner, Pool Green, Greenhill and others. The stile (right) led into Poulsom's farm.

Idyllic 1909 postcard entitled 'Neston Schools, Corshamside'. The school was built in 1861 as Corshamside School and enlarged in 1885. It appears to have been taken on a lazy summer's afternoon.

Corshamside (Neston) village lies several miles south of Corsham. This is Chapel lane. This Chapel is one of the first Open Brethren Assembly halls in the country. It was built on a small plot of land donated by Mr. Edridge who died before it was completed. It is dedicated to the Gospel of Jesus Christ to this day. The postcard was posted from Corsham to Bath by B. Oatley, one of the believers in 1911.

1950 postcard of St. Philip and St. James Neston. The church was opened on May 27th 1866 at Corshamside. J. H. Hakewill designed the church in the Early English style. It was constructed in locally quarried stone and comprises a nave, chancel and belfry. The parish register dates from 1868.

Soldiers of the Royal Artillery form a group on the side of the road in Neston in 1915.
Two are officers, four are sergeants. There are also bombardiers who had been in the
army for some time and were not new recruits. This super 'moment in time' was recorded
by the camera of Herbert Spackman. How many were killed in action?

A rare business card for the Neston Glove factory. Samuel Davis was well known and
attended the Gospel Hall. The Factory was established by Mr. G.P. Fuller of Neston Park
in 1906 in his barn. It was situated on the corner of Rough Street. Sheepskins were
'dressed' in preparation for glove cutting. At its height in the 1950's it was employing
over a hundred people. Note the nest in the hand trademark.

Neston School c. 1923. Laura Smith (teacher) stands with left to right: (back: Bessie Gale, Kathleen Light, Gladys Love, Francis Hemmings, Joan Smith, ?, Graham Light, Wilf Fidler. (middle:Chris Poulsom, ? Gatley, ?, ? Duckett, Winifred Gale, Percy Lodge, Ernie Smith. (front): Joyce Duckett, ?, Eunice Gainey, Olive Gale, Peggy Love, Jesse Light, Eva Lodge, John Poulsom, Marjorie Hemming.

May Day c.1938, taken on the Westwells road opposite the old co-op. On the float are the May Queen, Helen Jones, Nancy Hayward, Edony Jones and a little girl, appropriately named May. Maypole dancing was common across England and Neston would have been no exception to the merriment enjoyed by local families.

Neston Club and Institute in 1922. This photograph records the team's triumph as the winners of the Chippenham & District Skittle League. The captain sits proudly holding the winner's cup and the skittles and balls are set out to complete the picture. None of these men have yet been identified. Can you help? If so visit www.corshampostcards.com

Neston Club and Institute football team c. 1930. There are only 10 players. It is possibly the Melksham league. Left to Right: Front Row: ? Hand, Billy Bollen, ?, ?, ?Middle: Francis May, Gilbert Atkins, ? Hand, William Watts, Francis Light. Back: Jim Phelps, ? Cooke, Ernest Helps, Sid Cooke, ?, ?, Ernest Lodge, George White. Photo by Riddick of Melksham.

NESTON SCHOOL HOUSE, 8. A. M.

A delightful postcard posted from Corsham in 1912. It shows Mr Holloway of Neston delivering the post to Neston School. The caption even has the time; 8 A.M! Notice his walking cane and his dog standing on the wall. The school was built in 1861 as Corshamside School and enlarged in 1885. During World War II, it educated evacuees from vulnerable cities.

MOOR GREEN.   12331.

Moor Green showing the Congregational Chapel in 1937. The Chapel was built in 1833 at a cost of £100. The buildings in this area were constructed from locally quarried 'Bath' stone.

110

The Ridge Cricket Team c.1925. Back (Arthur Poulsom). L - R: (back row): Frank Indge, 'Bill' Sheppard, Frere Salmon, Frank Bollen. (middle): Stanley Poulsom, Cecil Archer, Stanley Gregory, 'Jack' Jones. (front): Gordon Indge, 'Eddie' Bollen, 'Ernie' Sheppard.

Neston Church Lads Brigade c. 1950. The area shield clearly shows the letters 'C. L. B'. It was taken outside the Neston Memorial Hall. In the front row (left) is Jim Carpenter. Others present are Ron Stannard, Jimmy Hancock, Harold Butler, Len Holloway, Stanley Gibbons, Rev. E.T. Davis and two commanders from Bristol. Can you identify the other lads? If so, visit www.corshampostcard.com

Neston House c.1908. This mansion has been synonymous with the Fuller family for over 200 years. The Fullers were great benefactors and central to Neston life. The 'Squire' G.P. Fuller (1833-1927), was a first class cricketer and M.P. for Wiltshire. In 1897 he built the Neston Club and Institute and in 1906 opened a Glove Factory. He was succeeded by his eldest son J.M.F. Fuller M.P.

Neston estate workers c.1928 on a postcard photograph by Herbert Spackman of Corsham. The Fullers of Neston Park have been at the heart of Neston life since 1790. It is possible that the gentleman in white (left) is J.M.F. Fuller M.P. Can anyone identify the exact location, the people or reason the photograph was taken?

112

MR & MRS G.P. FULLER. JAN. 1914.

A commemorative photograph of Mr and Mrs G.P. Fuller on the occasion of their Golden Wedding in January 1914. Fuller was educated at Winchester and Oxford where he won acclaim as a first class cricketer. He succeeded his father to the Neston Estate in 1872. He was an M.P. for 10 years after the General Election of 1885. G.P. Fuller was a key figure in the Neston district throughout his productive life.

On the back of this postcard is written '1st camp of the 2nd British at Neston Park Wilts.' It shows a group of scouts lining up to be served food with one of their tents in the background. Baden Powell established the first scouting camp on Brownsea Island in 1907 and in 1908 wrote 'Scouting for Boys'. G.P. Fuller (1833-1927) of Neston Park characteristically encouraged scout camps on his estate.

Neston Park.

Neston House in 1911. This fine Georgian mansion was built for John Fuller in 1803. The Fullers have lived here for over 200 years. The Fullers gave their name to Fullers Ales based in Chiswick in London. In 1916 Fullers established an Agricultural Society which supplied farm produce from a barn at Atworth.

WEST WILTS ELECTION, 1910.

Houlton, Trowbridge.]

Your vote and interest are respectfully solicited on behalf of

J. M. F. FULLER, ESQ.,

who has faithfully represented you since 1900, and who seeks a renewal of your kind confidence.

Sir John Michael Fleetwood Fuller (1864-1915) on an election canvassing postcard for the West Wilts Election 1910. Sir John was successful in being elected as M.P. for Westbury.

He was born on 21 October 1864 the eldest son of George Pargiter Fuller and Emily Georgina Jane Hicks-Beach. He married Norah Jacintha Phipps, daughter of Charles Phipps, on 5 July 1898. He died on 4 September 1915, aged 50.

This is now journey's end. I hope that you have enjoyed this historical tour of Corsham and its locality.

To view the whole collection or to purchase additional copies of this and other books online visit www.corshampostcards.com

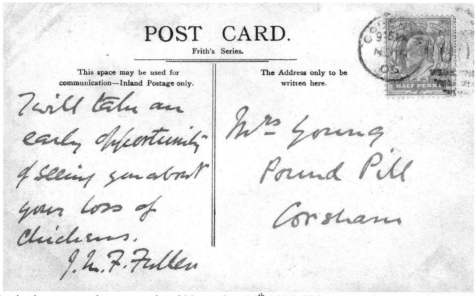

Intriguing postcard message dated November 15th 1905. This postcard was sent by J.M.F. Fuller to Mrs Young of Pound Pill Corsham on a picture of Jaggards House. *"I will take an early opportunity of seeing you about your loss of chickens".* Did it involve a fox?

The Author

Stephen Flavin is married with three children and lives in Chippenham. He was born in Corsham in 1961 and attended St. Patrick's R.C. Aided School on the day it opened. After leaving Corsham Comprehensive School, he studied music at King Alfred's College in Winchester. Stephen has taught at a number of secondary schools in Basingstoke, Bath and Yate. He is now the Headteacher of Churchfields Secondary School in Swindon.

Stephen's interest in the history of Corsham and district has resulted in the largest known collection of Edwardian postcards of Corsham. This entire collection can be viewed on a fascinating website called:
www.corshampostcards.com